ESCAPE
LONDON

Written by
SONYA BARBER

Grantchester Meadows (no.19)

INFORMATION IS DEAD.
LONG LIVE OPINION.

We love London. We hate London. Argh, the agony.

Put it this way: to really appreciate this city, you need to escape its gravitational pull every once in a while. Life outside it can seem so much saner. As a publisher, we make books that celebrate London, but we also know its limitations. This, then, is our unashamedly opinionated guide to the places we'd recommend you go if you came to us, heady on car fumes, in dire need of escape. This isn't an exhaustive list. It doesn't cover every county. It's *our* list: personally selected with our expert writer, Sonya Barber. Because, in the chaos of the capital, simplicity can be just what you need.

Our other opinionated guides:

East London

London Architecture

Vegan London

London Green Spaces

Independent London

London Pubs

Sweet London

Kids' London

This page: Rock-a-Nore beach (no.44)
Opposite: The medieval town of Rye (no.37)

River Lee Country Park (no. 13)

Charleston (no. 39)

SURE, LONDON IS GREAT...

But you know what can also be really excellent? Leaving it. (I mean just for a day or three – you won't find me moving to Margate quite yet.) As a born and bred Londoner, I'm used to being spoiled for choice when it comes to food, culture and fun, yet I'm increasingly finding I want to spend my weekends outside the M25. And I know it's not just me: lockdowns have made us all crave green spaces and sea air like never before, but we've always needed a break from the Big Smoke now and then to reset, refresh and relax. Changing your landscape can instantly change your mood. Being surrounded by fields instead of flats and swimming in lakes rather than lidos can banish existential dread like nothing else. And why are pubs so much cosier when they're in the countryside?

Luckily, you don't have to travel for long to feel very far away from the thrum of city life. Day trips are easier than you think: you can set off to get sand in your socks or admire an ancient forest and still be back in the capital in time for last orders. This book will introduce you to our favourite places in London's outer orbit: the restaurants and galleries that rival the capital's, the quirky hidden landscapes to discover and the hotels that offer much more than just a place to stay.

Instead of giving you a whole load of strict itineraries (where would be the fun in that?), we've picked 45 stand-out spots each worth a visit in their own right – and included some tips for exploring the surrounding area. Pick one and head straight there for a spontaneous day out, string together a few for a cheeky weekend break or tick off a whole bunch on a wild week away. And you don't need a car to get there – each place is within two hours of a mainline London train station (including, in some cases, a bus or short taxi ride on the other side).

So go on, what are you waiting for? Whether you choose to frolic through sweet-smelling fields of lavender (no.6) or cross a surreal shingle desert (no.29), peruse the menu at an oyster shack in the middle of the woods (no.2) or at a Michelin-starred pub (no.30 or no.33), explore a secret sculpture park (no.18) or brave a bracing wild swim (no.1), it's time to escape London. Bon voyage.

Sonya Barber, 2022

AREAS TO ESCAPE TO

Just beyond London (no.1–14)
You really don't have to go far
from the capital to escape city
life. Amid the suburban sprawl,
the outer London fringes and
home counties are full of
sublime green spaces, historic
architecture and arty diversions
– if you know where to look.

Around Oxford (no.15–18)
Dodge cyclists and *Harry Potter*
tours on your stroll around
Oxford's historic colleges and
libraries, then head away from
the dreaming spires to lose
yourself amid the blissful
English greenery of the
Cotswolds and Chilterns.

Around Cambridge (no.19–21)
Surrounded by flat East Anglian
fenland, Cambridge is a city of
university towers and medieval
streets – but also cool cafés, great
arts venues and plentiful greenery along the lazy River Cam.

Essex Coast (no.22–25)
Away from Essex's notorious
nightlife, you're in for a surprise
on the county's rough and
brooding coastline, where
golden sandy beaches, marshy
islands and picture-book
villages await.

Kent Coast (no.26–35)
The exodus of Londoners to
Margate, Whitstable and
Folkestone has led to a whole
host of new hotspots from
galleries to gastropubs, yet these
towns still retain their old-
school seaside charm.

Sussex Coast (no.36–45)
Brighton has always been a
beloved escape for Londoners,
but it's worth exploring every
inch of Sussex's south-facing
coastline, where pebble beaches
and majestic cliffs give way to
rolling downland, intriguing
towns and artistic attractions.

BEST FOR...

A long weekend

Spend a few days at Tillingham (no.38) and, when you're not sampling their tasty wines, venture out for walks around Rye Harbour Nature Reserve (no.37) and Dungeness (no.29). Or use Elmley Nature Reserve (no.32) as your base for dinner at Wheelers Oyster Bar (no.31) in Whitstable or go in search of the legendary tasting menu at The Sportsman (no.33). Birch (no.11) meanwhile offers a country weekend on the edge of London, where you can wander through Epping Forest (no.2) and River Lee Country Park (no.13).

A day at the seaside

For sea, sand and sunshine (the latter sadly not guaranteed), head to ever-so-cute Broadstairs to savour a scoop of Morelli's gelato (no.27) on the beach, Brighton Palace Pier (no.40) for classic arcade games and unexpected wildlife displays, Southend Pier (no.24) to stretch your legs or West Wittering Beach (no.45) for miles of uninterrupted white sand.

Art and culture

Any seaside town worth its salt has a landmark art gallery these days: tick off Margate's Turner Contemporary (no.26), Eastbourne's Towner (no.41) and Bexhill's De La Warr Pavilion (no.36). Inland, stroll around the homes of modernist masters at Charleston (no.39), the Henry Moore Foundation (no.4) and Kettle's Yard (no.21).

Country walks

For a cultural amble, head to Runnymede and stroll across the meadows to Writ in Water (no.3) or take in the sculptures at Albion Fields (no.18).

A more challenging constitutional (with great views as an incentive) can be had up West Wycombe Hill (no.16) or Box Hill (no.14). For a truly epic hike, tackle a chunk of the South Downs Way (no.42).

Food worth travelling for

Kent is the place for gastropub nirvana, with The Sportsman (no.33), The Fordwich Arms (no.30) and The Rose (no.34) all waiting to expand your waistline. Further west, Heckfield Place (no.7) and Thyme (no.17) offer fine dining with heart and homegrown ingredients, while in Essex BYOB seafood shack The Company Shed (no.25) serves up exquisite platters at the opposite end of the budget spectrum.

Family days out

The fields of fruit and veg at Parkside Pick Your Own (no.5) or the tiny world of Bekonscot Model Village (no.12) just outside of London will keep kids (and adults) entertained for a few precious hours. For a full day out, venture further afield to the ramparts of Bodiam Castle (no.43).

Places for a dip

You've heard of the benefits of cold-water swimming, now take the plunge. For calm sea swims, nothing beats Walpole Bay Tidal Pool (no.28) in Margate. If refreshing rivers are more your thing, take a dip at Port Meadow (no.15) or Grantchester Meadows (no.19). Or for gentle lake laps, try Frensham Great Pond (no.1) or Heckfield Place (no.7).

Something a bit different

If you've traipsed around enough National Trust properties to last you a lifetime, switch it up with the eccentric, hand-painted interiors of Charleston (no.39) or the David Parr House (no.20). Or, for unusual landscapes, try the alien panorama of Dungeness (no.29), the offbeat follies of Painshill (no.8), or the wonderfully weird sight of Grayson Perry's A House for Essex (no.22) perched above the Stour Estuary.

1

FRENSHAM GREAT POND

South London's closest 'beach'

In Surrey's luscious greenery lies this not-so-hidden gem: a sprawling freshwater bathing spot complete with sandy beach. On hot weekends, Frensham Great Pond is bustling with locals and clued-up Londoners, taking a dip or relaxing among the sand dunes. But visit on a greyer day and you're likely to only be sharing the beach with ducks, swooping swallows, horse riders and the occasional hardy wild swimmer. It's a truly bucolic spot that feels like a real discovery. All that's missing is the sea.

Farnham, GU10 2QB
Waterloo to Farnham, then taxi or bus
waverley.gov.uk

2

EPPING FOREST

Ancient woodland at the end of the Central line

Stretching from east London up into Essex, Epping Forest is an epic labyrinth of centuries-old oaks, beeches, birches and hornbeams. Regular visitors each have their own preferred patch: whether it's the open spaces at Chingford Plain, the Iron Age hill fort of Loughton Camp or the bluebell woods at Wanstead Park. In this magical place, the subject of generations of folklore, you might stumble across the fabled cave said to have been highwayman Dick Turpin's hide-out or find yourself on the banks where Queen Boudicca once allegedly made camp. After meandering through myths, refresh yourself at the Original Tea Hut – a legend in itself that's been serving up proper brews since 1930 – or with a scallop-and-bacon butty at the Oyster Shack & Seafood Bar.

Visitor centre: Loughton, IG10 4AF
⊖ *Loughton*
visiteppingforest.org

3

WRIT IN WATER

*Architectural installation on
the site of Magna Carta*

Hankering after a stroll with a spot of culture?
Look no further than artist Mark Wallinger's 2017
installation, Writ in Water: a looming rotunda made
from compacted earth plonked in the middle of a
field. Not just any field though: tranquil Runnymede
meadow was the site of the pioneering medieval
treaty, Magna Carta, which laid the groundwork
for modern democracy. Step inside Wallinger's
structure and you'll follow a dark passage towards
a bright inner sanctum, where an inscription from
Magna Carta reflects on-to a shallow pool. Once
you're done pondering the weight of history, lighten
the mood with a stroll to the National Trust café
for a proper cream tea.

Egham, TW20 0LG
⇌ *Waterloo to Egham*
nationaltrust.org.uk

exiled, or deprived of his standing in any way

4

HENRY MOORE FOUNDATION

Sculpture, greenery and a powerful artistic legacy

Day-trippers en route to the pretty Hertfordshire hamlet of Perry Green usually have one motive in mind: admiring massive bronze sculptures. The artist Henry Moore and his wife Irina lived here for more than 40 years, scattering studios, out-buildings and chunky sculpted forms across their ever-expanding idyllic grounds. Wander through the lawns, fields and wooded trails today and you can scope out 20 monumental sculptures, includ-ing the aptly named Large Reclining Figure loom-ing menacingly on a hillock. You can also poke around Moore's house, Hoglands, his studio full of artistic bric-a-brac and an ancient barn full of tapestries (but take note: the whole site closes through winter).

Perry Green, SG10 6EE
⇌ Liverpool St to Bishop's Stortford, then taxi
henry-moore.org

5

PARKSIDE FARM PICK YOUR OWN

Fill a basket with seasonally grown goodies

Always fancied an allotment but can't face the weeding, or the waiting list? At this 50-acre farm on the edge of London, you get to pick the fruits of other people's labours. From May to October, you can grab a punnet, a bag or a whole trolley and fill it with whatever's in season – including strawberries, raspberries, courgettes and broad beans in summer, and squash, sweetcorn or black-berries in autumn. Your fruit and veg gets weighed (and very reasonably priced, with your entry fee deducted) at the end in the farm shop, where you can also pick up a jar of the farm's own honey or a pot of local cream for your strawberries. Bring a child if you have one – they really help with the low-hanging fruit.

Parkside Farm, EN2 8LA
⊖ *Cockfosters, then bus or taxi*
parksidefarmpyo.co.uk

6

MAYFIELD LAVENDER

A panorama of purple in London's green belt

Who needs the South of France when fragrant fields of lavender grow in deepest south London? Visit Mayfield during peak season, from July to early August, and it's hard not to be overwhelmed by the sheer purple potency of its annual crop. It's paradise for flower-lovers, bumblebees and Instagram influencers alike (though don't worry, with 25 acres to explore, there's plenty of space to avoid photobombing any selfies). Picking the flowers is strictly forbidden, but there's a great-smelling gift shop where you can gather armfuls of organic soap, essential oils and fresh or dried bouquets. If that's just not enough of the stuff, stop by the café for a lavender-infused cream tea.

Banstead, SM7 3JA
≽ London Bridge to Purley, then bus or taxi
mayfieldlavender.com

7

HECKFIELD PLACE

Contemporary country-house hotel
with foodie credentials

The new owners of this once-neglected stately home in Hampshire spent almost an entire decade primping and preening it into a hotel – and boy, does it show. Serious care and creativity (not to mention cash) has gone into pretty much everything you'll encounter here, from the modern art on the walls to the grandiose underground cinema. As for activities: you can roam the massive grounds at will, take a dip in the lake, join a forest-bathing walk or pick fruit on the farm. But ultimately the biggest draw here is the food – expect sensational, seasonal fare from dawn till dusk, all overseen by Michelin-star chef Skye Gyngell.

Heckfield, RG27 0LD
Waterloo to Winchfield, then taxi
heckfieldplace.com

8

PAINSHILL

Fantastical landscape of follies and foliage

Back in the 18th century, aristocrats went wild for extravagant gardens designed to look like living paintings, full of useless (but beautiful) ornamental structures. Not many still exist – but one such masterpiece has survived tucked away in the Surrey countryside. Walk the three-mile 'historic route' through the Hon. Charles Hamilton's eccentric creation at Painshill and you'll spot a gothic tower, a Turkish tent, a Greek temple and a ruined abbey all nestling among the meticulously planted gardens. The highlight is a subterranean lakeside grotto, dripping with crystal stalactites, but the whole site is a surreal yet pastoral experience – where the only thing that reminds you that you're not dreaming is the low hum of the A3.

Cobham, KT11 1BE

⇌ *Waterloo to Cobham & Stoke d'Abernon, then bus or taxi*

painshill.co.uk

9

ALL SAINTS'
CHURCH, TUDELEY

Uniquely spectacular stained-glass windows

It's usually worth popping inside an English country church if you're passing, but this one in the Kent countryside deserves a trip of its own. It's the only church in the world to have all of its windows designed by modernist artist Marc Chagall, who was commissioned to create a single memorial pane but announced on arrival: 'It's magnificent. I will do them all.' Chagall's elongated forms float through the vivid glow of blue, yellow and pink glass – you can even spot individual brushstrokes and his scrawled signature, and it's easy to spend a peaceful hour pointing out angels, birds and butterflies. Make a day of it with one of the many rambling routes that lead out from the village, finishing up back at Tudeley's gastropub, The Poacher and Partridge.

Tudeley, TN11 0NZ
⇒ *Charing Cross to Tonbridge, then bus or taxi*
tudeley.org

10

THAMES LIDO

A dip worthy of a day trip

Picture this: you're sitting by a sparkling pool in a fluffy robe, scoffing Ibérico ham. No, you're not at a fancy hotel in Spain, but an Edwardian lido in (hopefully) sunny Reading. Colourfully restored in 2017 after years of neglect, thanks to a successful community campaign, Thames Lido now entices bathers from near and far. Not only is its 25-metre heated pool an inordinately picturesque place for a spot of breaststroke, but the al fresco hot tub, spa treatment rooms using all-natural products and onsite tapas bar mean you can make a mini-holiday of it – while only travelling half an hour from central London.

Reading, RG1 8FR
⇌ Paddington to Reading
thameslido.com

11

BIRCH

Grand hotel and grown-ups' playground

Legend has it that the 19th-century socialite who once owned this 55-acre estate used to ride around London in a carriage drawn by zebras. These days, Birch channels that spirit of eccentricity into a sprawling country-house hotel with the air of a boutique festival. Why stick to just lying by the lido or having dinner at Robin Gill's excellent restaurant, when you could also join a spoon-whittling circle, pottery workshop or outdoor yoga class? Catch a film from a deckchair in one of the ballrooms, book a fire pit for an al fresco cook-off, or (if you must) check your emails in the workspace – which turns into a buzzing members' bar after dark. It feels simultaneously very far away from London, and very Shoreditch.

Cheshunt, EN7 5HW
≽ Liverpool St to Theobalds Grove, then taxi
birchcommunity.com

12

BEKONSCOT MODEL VILLAGE

A nostalgic world in miniature

There's only one place near London where you can visit a castle, a zoo, a funfair and a fishing village all in the space of an hour. The catch? They're all about 12 inches high. Bekonscot, the world's oldest model village, opened in 1929 and claims to have since welcomed more than 15 million (full-sized) people to gawp at its recreations of interwar England. Here you'll find life, death and everything in between: there's peril (a house on fire), merriment (Morris dancers), industry (coal mines and factories), and a whole load of pun-tastic shop names. Linking it all is a sprawling model railway that whizzes through scaled-down stations – and if you need to distract your little ones from trying to grab the buildings, Godzilla-style, there's a (slightly) larger train they can ride, too.

Beaconsfield, HP9 2PL
⇌ *Marylebone to Beaconsfield*
bekonscot.co.uk

13

RIVER LEE
COUNTRY PARK

1,000 acres of countryside on London's doorstep

In need of a quick nature fix? A 20-minute train ride from the City, this sprawl of meadows, woods and waterways awaits. Pick any route from Cheshunt station and you'll soon find yourself wandering alongside lakes and rivers, over bridges and past narrowboats, surrounded by swooping birds and flitting dragonflies. You could pack a picnic and find a shady spot under the trees, bring bikes and cycle up the Lee Navigation towpath, or hire a canoe and take to the water. Whatever you do, finish at The Crown pub near Broxbourne for a riverside pint before catching the train back into town.

Cheshunt, EN8 9AJ
⇌ *Liverpool St to Cheshunt*
visitleevalley.org.uk

14

BOX HILL

Hike towards the Surrey Hills' classic vista

Attracting hordes of Londoners since at least the 18th century, this beauty spot was a favourite day-trip destination long before it featured in Jane Austen's *Emma*. The lovely walk (around an hour) from Box Hill & Westhumble station takes you across a famous set of stepping stones, up a steep climb and back along the ridge, with spectacular views over quintessentially English countryside all the way. Once you reach the summit, reward yourself with tea and cake at the well-placed National Trust café. The strong-thighed might fancy the cycle up Zig Zag Road – which has become Surrey's answer to Mont Ventoux since its inclusion in the 2012 Olympics – or if that sounds nothing like your idea of fun, perhaps you might prefer a tour and tasting at nearby Denbies Wine Estate?

Tadworth, KT20 7LB
⇌ *Victoria to Box Hill & Westhumble then walk or taxi*
nationaltrust.org.uk

15

PORT MEADOW

Ancient common for wild swims and walks

There are plenty of reasons people visit Oxford: its historic colleges, its medieval streets or its plethora of *Harry Potter* filming locations. But on its north-western fringes lies another world. Port Meadow is an ancient stretch of common land alongside the River Thames (or the River Isis, as it's known here). In summer, the fields attract locals and students, and the river is a beloved bathing spot. In winter, it's a dramatic place for a wander as the land floods and fills with birdlife. Don't mind the resident cows and horses – they're more than used to curious humans. Plus, opportunities for pub detours abound: decamp to The Perch's famous riverside beer garden, or grab a seat by the fire at The Old Bookbinders.

Oxford, OX2 6ED
⇌ *Paddington to Oxford*
oxford.gov.uk

16

WEST WYCOMBE

Historic village with a devilish past

Deep in the otherwise respectable Chilterns, the time-warp village of West Wycombe is famous for once being the home of 18th-century libertine Sir Francis Dashwood, founder of the so-called Hellfire Club: a high-society circle whose members were rumoured to worship the devil. Francis and his fiendish friends used to meet at West Wycombe for sordid, claret-fuelled parties, which took place in a series of chalk caves dug into West Wycombe Hill. Nowadays you can visit the Dashwood family's stately home and grounds, then descend into the creepy passages and echoing chambers of the Hellfire Caves. Once you emerge, climb up to the enormous mausoleum that Sir Francis built for himself on the panoramic summit, then head to The Swan Inn in the village for some obligatory carousing.

West Wycombe, HP14 3AE
⇌ Marylebone to High Wycombe, then taxi or bus
nationaltrust.org.uk

17

THYME

Family-run Cotswolds bolthole
celebrating nature

If your idea of the Cotswolds is honey-coloured houses, rolling fields and farm-fresh food, Thyme will tick all your boxes. Billing itself as 'a village within a village', this luxurious hotel in Southrop has a strong emphasis on all things local and natural, with its own barn restaurant, boutique shop, spa, kitchen garden, spring-water pool and even an ivy-clad pub. Its country-chic rooms are scattered across various cottages, outbuildings and farmhouses, with views over manicured gardens and fields full of stylish black sheep. You'll probably want to leave any kids at home: Thyme is a grown-up escape where children aren't allowed. But if you can't find a babysitter for the weekend, sprogs (and dogs) can stay in the delightfully chintzy Old Walls cottage on the edge of the estate.

Southrop, GL7 3NX
⇌ *Paddington to Swindon, then taxi*
thyme.co.uk

18

ALBION FIELDS

Secret sculpture park in the verdant Thames valley

A massive metal sculpture of an inflated car might be the last thing you'd expect to see on the driveway of a quaint Oxfordshire farm. But it makes sense when you find out that this is the home of Michael Hue-Williams, an art dealer and gallerist whose phone book clearly isn't short on big names. Having converted an outbuilding into an acclaimed gallery space in 2013, Hue-Williams has now gone one better by turning his 50-acre estate in sleepy Little Milton into a cutting-edge contemporary sculpture park, which partners with top London galleries on ever-changing al fresco exhibitions. Booking a slot (each Friday and Saturday) entitles you to wander the fields and woods at your leisure, scratching your head at intriguing works by artists such as Ai Weiwei and Richard Long.

Little Milton, OX44 7QB
Coach: Oxford Tube from Victoria to Lewknor Turn, then taxi
albionbarn.com

19

GRANTCHESTER MEADOWS

Cambridge's riverside paradise

There aren't many wild swimming spots with a pedigree like this one: its artistic visitors over the years have included Lord Byron, Virginia Woolf, Sylvia Plath and Pink Floyd. The River Cam meanders through the fields here for more than a mile, from Skaters' Meadow to Byron's Pool, drifting past roaming cows and lounging students. Find a way down to the water along the muddy riverbanks, and you're in for a blissful dip. Bring a picnic so you can settle in for the day once you've emerged, or stop for a pint at The Blue Ball Inn before taking the scenic route back across the meadows into town.

Cambridge, CB3 9JN
⇜ *King's Cross to Cambridge, then taxi*
cambridge.gov.uk

20

DAVID PARR HOUSE

Ornately muralled artist's house

Most people don't like to bring their work home, but Victorian decorative painter David Parr wasn't most people. Over the course of almost half a century, he obsessively covered virtually every inch of the walls and ceiling in his cramped, terraced home with elaborate designs – painted flowers, geometric patterns, gothic-lettered scrolls and stained glass – all while raising a family and working for a local decorator's firm. His work lives on thanks to his late granddaughter, Elsie, who herself lived here for 85 years, keeping Parr's murals (and his dusty cupboard full of paint pots) mostly intact. The house opened to the public in 2019, with Elsie's possessions – including her collection of hot water bottle stoppers – still dotted around. Book on to one of the small group tours for a *Through the Keyhole* like no other.

Cambridge, CB1 2LW
≽ *King's Cross to Cambridge*
davidparrhouse.org

21

KETTLE'S YARD

Curator's cottage turned art gallery

Once the home of British art collector Jim Ede, today Kettle's Yard is possibly England's most aesthetically pleasing exhibition space. Not only is it packed with important modernist paintings and sculptures, it's also a source of endless interior design inspiration, with its whitewashed walls, abundant houseplants and precisely arranged pebble displays. There's even a single fresh lemon on a pewter plate, replaced daily, that mirrors a yellow dot in a nearby Miró painting. By the time you've wandered through the ancient buildings and expansive upper galleries, you'll have serious house envy as well as the feeling you've been artistically nourished.

Cambridge, CB3 0AQ
⇌ *King's Cross to Cambridge*
kettlesyard.co.uk

22

A HOUSE FOR ESSEX

Eccentric architectural artwork

Thanks to the rather rare booking opportunities and undimming demand, chances are you won't be spending the night in Grayson Perry's eccentric folly above the sweeping Stour Estuary. Luckily, there's plenty to appreciate from the outside. A circular walk from the village of Wrabness down to the water goes right past it, letting you ogle the handmade geometric tiles and roof sculptures through which Perry tells the story of a fictional Essex girl, Julie Cope. The building resembles a fairy-tale gingerbread house, particularly at sunset when rays glint off the pitched golden roof. See if you can catch a glimpse of the murals inside through the huge, arched windows, then carry on down to the water for a picturesque stroll or a picnic overlooking the estuary.

Wrabness, CO11 2TP
⮆ Liverpool St to Wrabness
living-architecture.co.uk

23

DEDHAM VALE

Essex's loveliest landscape

Dedham Vale is far from a secret: this Area of Outstanding Natural Beauty's car parks are unceasingly busy with day-trippers exploring 'Constable Country'. But don't let that put you off. Start in the tiny village of Dedham, where the high street boasts a plethora of wisteria-covered houses, a tearoom and a few foodie pubs. Find a spot in the garden of the cosy Sun Inn, where you can play a game of boules between sips of local ales. From Dedham, an easy circular walking route towards Flatford Mill takes you through the bucolic landscape along the River Stour. On sunny days it's a great place for a wild swim – just be careful of the amateur rowers wobbling down from The Boathouse restaurant, which offers an unusual 'row and dine' package.

Dedham, CO7 6DH
⇌ Liverpool St to Manningtree, then taxi
dedhamvalestourvalley.org

24

SOUTHEND PIER

Record-breaking Essex landmark

Southenders aren't shy of boasting about the size of their pleasure pier – and nor should they be: at over a mile long, it's officially the world's longest. The unbeatable views from the end over the Thames Estuary are well worth the trek (though do make sure you're wearing comfortable shoes). Alternatively, you can hop aboard the antique mini-railway that clatters all the way to the end and back. Whether you walked or not, reward yourself afterwards with an old-school knickerbocker glory from nearby Rossi's ice-cream parlour. Then, if you've still got the energy, set out along the esplanade towards nearby Leigh-on-Sea, where fish and chips and fishermen's pubs await.

Southend-on-Sea, SS1 1EE
⇌ Fenchurch St to Southend Central
southendpier.co.uk

25

THE COMPANY SHED

*Fresher-than-fresh seafood on an
enchanting island*

There are plenty of places to sample the daily
catch off the British coast, but those in the know
always come back to a certain unassuming beach
shack on Mersea Island. From local oysters to tiger
prawns, the menu at The Company Shed changes
every day depending on what the boats have
brought in, but whatever ends up on the colossal
seafood platters here, it's always as fresh as it comes.
(Plus you can bring your own booze – and bread.)
Elsewhere on the island there are beaches, coastal
walks and even a vineyard. Just make sure to time
your visit right: the causeway from the Essex main-
land gets swallowed up at high tide.

West Mersea, CO5 8PA
⇌ Liverpool St to Colchester, then bus or taxi
thecompanyshed.co

26

TURNER CONTEMPORARY

Pioneering art gallery beside the sea

Long before Margate became the default seaside destination for east Londoners, lured by its vintage theme park and stream of foodie new openings, the Turner Contemporary was attracting culture-lovers from near and far. Although it's not the biggest space, it punches above its weight with an acclaimed programme of free exhibitions, showing work by Steve McQueen, Martin Parr, Tracey Emin and Sarah Lucas (plus the bronze Antony Gormley figure staring off into the waves outside). The building itself is a beauty too, and the sea wall right behind it is a great spot to watch the blazing sunsets that drew painter J.M.W. Turner to Margate time and time again. Book a seafood supper at Angela's to round off your day at the seaside in style.

Margate, CT9 1HG
St Pancras to Margate
turnercontemporary.org

27

MORELLI'S GELATO

Retro ice-cream parlour for a seaside sugar rush

Huddled around a quaint horseshoe bay, Broadstairs is Kent's quintessential seaside resort – even Charles Dickens used to come here for a paddle. This place has it all: beach huts, amusement arcades, a bandstand, and, of course, the retro splendour of Morelli's ice-cream parlour. Step inside this pastel-pink 1960s time-capsule for towering sundaes made with their famous fresh gelato, or choose a scoop from the likes of Piemonte hazelnut, Sicilian pistachio and Sorrento lemon sorbet, then take your cone across the road to devour in Victoria Gardens while you gaze out over the sandy beach below. Whatever you pick, leave room for lunch at seafood specialist Wyatt and Jones or at the town's liveliest local pub, Neptunes Hall.

Broadstairs, CT10 1QS
⇌ *St Pancras to Broadstairs*
morellisgelato.com

28

WALPOLE BAY TIDAL POOL

A concrete paradise for open-air swimmers

A short walk from central Margate, underneath a towering chalk cliff, the Walpole Bay Tidal Pool has been welcoming intrepid sea swimmers since 1937. Refilling with saltwater at each high tide, it provides calm conditions year-round, drawing crowds of families in summer and brave locals through winter. Wade in from the beach for a paddle or walk out (carefully) along the seaweed-covered concrete walls to lower yourself in at one of the rusty old ladders. After a few laps (or simply some time floating in the buoyant sea water), warm up with eggs and bagels at Cliffs on nearby Northdown Road, a classic afternoon tea at the eccentric Walpole Bay Hotel or a brisk stroll along the cliffs towards Botany Bay.

Margate, CT9 3AB
St Pancras to Margate, then walk or taxi
visitmargate.co.uk

29

DUNGENESS

The south coast's weirdest beachscape

The otherworldly expanse of shingle beach known as Dungeness is a bleak but beautiful place: a desert-like landscape in the shadow of a nuclear power station. Walk along the atmospheric foreshore, past beached fishing boats, lighthouses and a cluster of dwellings that range from crumbly shacks to sleek modernist cabins. (The most famous is Prospect Cottage, pictured right, the former home of cult film director Derek Jarman – you can still see his beloved pebble garden.) Then grab a pint at the Britannia Inn and watch the tiny trains of the Romney, Hythe and Dymchurch railway steam past.

Dungeness, TN29 9NB
⇌ London Bridge to Rye, then taxi
dungeness.org.uk

30

THE FORDWICH ARMS

A refined riverside pub for a real treat

There's posh pub grub aplenty in Kent (The Sportsman, no.33, is another fine example), but our pick for a seriously special occasion has got to be The Fordwich Arms. Right on the idyllic banks of the River Stour, this Michelin-starred spot is definitely not your average country boozer. The (incredible) six-course tasting menu celebrating local ingredients will set you back upwards of £100 per person, with a wine list bordering on the biblical. Be sure to book well in advance; ask for a table in the waterside terrace or garden, or inside by the fire in winter, and get ready for a memorable meal.

Fordwich, CT2 0DB
≋ St Pancras to Sturry
fordwicharms.co.uk

31

WHEELERS OYSTER BAR

Landmark seafood destination

Despite its recent reinvention as an artsy hub for ex-Londoners craving sea air, Whitstable is a fishing town at heart, with a bustling working harbour and seafood shacks aplenty. Oysters are so central to the town's identity that it even has an annual summer festival devoted to them – but year-round, there's no more historic place to indulge than Wheelers. Behind the restaurant's much-photographed, pastel-pink façade, not much has changed since it was founded by mariner Richard 'Leggy' Wheeler and his wife Mary-Ann in 1856. In its tiny, homely dining rooms lined with knick-knacks and nautical prints, Wheelers serves up unbelievably fresh seafood, from classic oysters and seafood platters to curried haddock fish-cakes and lobster lasagne. To top it all off, it's BYOB.

Whitstable, CT5 1BQ
⇌ St Pancras to Whitstable
wheelersoysterbar.com

Wheelers Oyster Bar

Whitstable

PHONE 27 3311

ALL
SEA
OODS

WHEELERS   OYSTER BAR

in or take away
OYSTERS
OCKLES
WHELKS
MUSSELS
EELS
PRAWNS
CRABS
OBSTERS
e our hot fish menu
in window?

AT WHEELERS
SALMON FISH CAKES
CRAB & PRAWN TOASTS
FISH FLANS
FISH PIES
LOCAL SHRIMPS
TODAY

OYSTERS
With BROWN BREAD
& BUTTER & LEMON
11/4 A DOZEN

Established 1856

OPEN

8

32

ELMLEY NATURE RESERVE

*The only British nature reserve where you
can stay overnight*

Compared to nearby Whitstable (see no.31), not many
Londoners day-tripping down to the Kentish seaside
make it to the Isle of Sheppey. But if you need one great
reason to visit, it's Elmley Nature Reserve. Occupying
a hefty chunk of the island (3,300 acres, to be precise)
its secluded, marshy landscape is home to more than
100 species of birds, mammals, reptiles, frogs, butterflies and bees. It's a great spot for a bird-watching walk,
but even better if you spend the night. As well as rooms
in the farmhouse (with dinner served in the majestic
barn next door), there are sumptuous shepherd's huts,
bell tents and impeccably designed cabins – some with
outdoor baths, so you can spot passing lapwings from
the tub.

Elmley, ME12 3RW
≥ *St Pancras to Swale, then taxi*
elmleynaturereserve.co.uk

33
THE SPORTSMAN

Michelin-starred fare in a friendly,
unassuming pub

It doesn't look like much from the outside – just another roadside pub next to a field – but The Sportsman is well worth the journey to the outskirts of Seasalter, near Whitstable. Why? Because it serves some of the best food in Kent in surroundings that are refreshingly down-to-earth. The five-course tasting menu might take you from local oysters to raspberry soufflé via venison and hake, but the atmosphere and service are as laidback and unstuffy as any local pub. It's no wonder tables get booked up months in advance, nor that the pub has held on to its Michelin star for well over a decade.

Seasalter, CT5 4BP
St Pancras to Faversham, then taxi
thesportsmanseasalter.co.uk

34
THE ROSE

Design-led foodie pub with rooms

Yes, the cottages in Deal's conservation area are exceptionally charming, and the promenade along the stony beach *is* very good for a wander, but lunch at The Rose is pretty much guaranteed to be the star of your visit to this trendy seaside town – especially if you can get a table in the Mediterranean-inspired courtyard garden on a sunny day. Renowned London chef Nuno Mendes has been collaborating on their menus since 2020; order his surprisingly savoury olive oil cake if you spot it. Upstairs are eight vintage-inspired bedrooms, making this a spot-on base to tour Deal, as well as the nearby picture-postcard streets of Sandwich or Kingsdown.

Deal, CT14 6ED
≽ *St Pancras to Deal*
therosedeal.com

35

FOLKESTONE HARBOUR ARM

Street-food market stretching out to sea

Throughout the last century, Folkestone's harbour arm thronged with packet steamers and cross-channel ferries. Nowadays the buzz comes from art and street food, and the only containers you'll find here are cartons full of halloumi fries, platters of fresh prawns and pints of Kentish craft beer. Stroll out along the walkway, looking out for the part-submerged Antony Gormley sculpture while grazing on vegan burgers, Dutch mussels or posh fish and chips from the resident food vendors, then stop off at the converted lighthouse for a glass of champagne, soul-stirring views along the cliffs and the chance to spot passing dolphins.

Folkestone, CT20 1QH
≋ *St Pancras to Folkestone Central*
folkestoneharbourarm.co.uk

36

DE LA WARR PAVILION

Art deco gallery and gig venue

Since reopening in 2005, this prominent seafront institution has made low-key Bexhill-on-Sea a cultural destination on the south coast. The spectacular, modernist, 1930s building is home to two galleries that host a wide range of contemporary art exhibitions, and there's a large events space that has welcomed everyone from Eddie Izzard and David Baddiel to the Pixies and Patti Smith. The fish and chips – served from the café and eaten on the waterside terrace – aren't bad either. Be sure to stop by the in-house record store, Music's Not Dead, to bring some of that culture home with you.

Bexhill-on-Sea, TN40 1DP
⇌ *Victoria to Bexhill*
dlwp.com

37

RYE HARBOUR NATURE RESERVE

Sweeping coastal marshland

The pretty, medieval town of Rye was once a bustling port, but now (thanks to coastal silting) it's more than a mile from the sea. However, once you've explored its cobbled streets and boutique shops, it's still well worth making the short trip to the tiny neighbouring seaside village of Rye Harbour, where the salt marshes of the nature reserve await. From there, stroll along the coast to Winchelsea Beach: it's an hour's walk under a huge sky through an almost alien landscape that's also one of England's richest natural habitats. Keep an eye out for wildlife as well as local landmarks, like the red-roofed fisherman's hut, the abandoned lifeboat house and the distant ramparts of Camber Castle.

Rye Harbour, TN31 7TU
⇒ London Bridge to Rye, then taxi
rye.sussexwildlifetrust.org.uk

38

TILLINGHAM

The UK's coolest vineyard

Natural wine has conquered London's drinking scene, and there's a vineyard just south of the capital well-known by wine fanatics for producing some of the UK's best: Tillingham. But even if you don't know your pét-nat from your supermarket plonk, Tillingham is a charming spot for a visit. Its impressive restaurant celebrates Sussex produce, and there's no need to leave after dinner: book into one of the stylish bedrooms in a converted former hops shed, where you can watch the sun set over the vines. Before you check out, buy a bottle (or a crate) of one of the house wines to savour later.

Peasmarsh, TN31 6XD
London Bridge to Rye, then taxi
tillingham.com

39

CHARLESTON

Hand-painted home of the Bloomsbury artists

Ever thought your love life was complicated? You've got nothing on Vanessa Bell and Duncan Grant. These two radical artists lived, worked and loved together at Charleston farmhouse for almost half a century, despite Bell being married and Grant mostly preferring men. They painted the walls and furniture with geometric patterns and saucy nudes, hosted wild Bloomsbury Group dinner parties (guests included Vanessa's sister Virginia Woolf) and cultivated a riotously colourful garden. The electric atmosphere still lingers today: as you wander through the rooms, it's like the residents have just stepped out, with their paintings, books and knick-knacks perfectly preserved. The house and garden are the main draw, but leave time to take in the temporary exhibitions and pick up some Bloomsbury-inspired décor in the thoughtfully curated shop.

Firle, BN8 6LL
🚆 *Victoria to Lewes, then taxi*
charleston.org.uk

40

BRIGHTON PALACE PIER

Seaside attractions – and a surprise natural wonder

A visit to Brighton isn't complete without a stroll on the pier – you can visit year-round for the sickly-sweet smell of frying doughnuts and the happy cacophony of arcade games and fairground rides. But there's a secret, magical spectacle that can only be glimpsed at dusk on winter evenings: a murmuration of hundreds of starlings, returning to their roosts under the pier. A cloud of birds swoops over and around the structure, in an unforgettable aerial sequence. It can easily be seen from the beach, but a spot on the pier itself gets you closer to the action as the flock builds to a breathtaking peak just after sunset.

Brighton, BN2 1TW
≈ Victoria to Brighton
brightonpier.co.uk

41

TOWNER EASTBOURNE

Eclectic gallery championing local artists

You can't miss the multicoloured façade of the Towner, which has been welcoming art lovers to Eastbourne since 1923. Despite this longevity, the gallery stays right up to date with shows by rising contemporary artists that rival any in London. But the Towner celebrates local talent as well, with exhibitions curated by prominent figures like Brighton MP Caroline Lucas and a whole room dedicated to Eastbourne-raised painter and printmaker Eric Ravilious. Aside from the art, there's also a cinema and a top-notch, top-floor café (though it can get a bit windy on the terrace: hold onto your hat). Once you're thoroughly arted out, you can rent an e-bike from Cadence Cycle Club over the road and take a tour of the town, ending with an ice cream at old-school seafront gelato parlour Fusciardi's.

Eastbourne, BN21 4JJ
⇌ Victoria to Eastbourne
townereastbourne.org.uk

42

SOUTH DOWNS WAY

100 miles of rural beauty

It would take you about nine days to hike the full length of the South Downs Way – the famously rugged footpath that follows the cliffs from Winchester to Beachy Head, crossing three counties along the way. But if you're planning more of a casual stroll than an epic pilgrimage, simply pick a scenic chunk of it instead. The sharp peaks of the Seven Sisters are a popular choice, with sea views just as breathtaking as the steep inclines. And there are plenty of more manageable stretches along the chalk ridges: all with superlative vistas and many accessible by public transport. Catch a bus from Brighton to Pyecombe or Eastbourne to Alfriston – or head to the market towns of Lewes and Petworth for cosy pubs, antiques shops, art galleries, and a chance to rest your aching feet.

≋ *Victoria or Waterloo to various destinations*
nationaltrail.co.uk

43

BODIAM CASTLE

Moated medieval fortress

Visiting an ancient castle should be on everyone's to-do list, and although there's no shortage of historic crenellations in the counties surrounding London, Bodiam Castle is the place to really get into the medieval spirit. With its looming square profile and vast moat, it looks every inch the imposing fortress. But once you're over the drawbridge and through the portcullis, you'll find a picturesque, partially restored ruin – with enough 'murder holes', spiral staircases and garderobes to thrill aspiring knights of any age. For extra excitement, arrive in steam-powered style via the Kent and East Sussex Railway, or by boat along the River Rother.

Robertsbridge, TN32 5UA
≼ *Charing Cross to Robertsbridge, then taxi*
nationaltrust.org.uk

44

ROCK-A-NORE

Bustling beach with myriad attractions

New York might have Rockaway Beach, but Hastings has Rock-a-Nore. This stretch of seafront near the Old Town has been a lively fisherman's landing place for more than a thousand years, and its towering, black-wood net sheds are still in use today. But there's plenty more to discover here – like the Hastings Contemporary gallery with its panoramic community café; a tiny aquarium where you can spot sharks and rays; quirky museums dedicated to shipwrecks and fishing history; and a 1940s miniature railway that big and little kids can ride a quarter-mile along the seafront. Once you're done exploring, catch the rattly Edwardian hill-lift up the cliff for a bracing walk over to secluded Fairlight Glen Beach.

Hastings, TN34 3DW
⇌ Charing Cross to Hastings
hastings.gov.uk

45

WEST WITTERING BEACH

The whitest sands in Sussex

Sandy beaches are sadly in short supply across most of South East England, so it's no wonder this sweeping shoreline is such a popular spot. Throughout autumn and winter, it's a hub for dog walkers, bird watchers and anyone craving a breezy beach walk. And although it does get intensely packed on hot summer weekends (book parking in advance and be sure to pack a picnic to avoid the queues), you'll always eventually find somewhere to pitch your blanket along the nearly two miles of dunes that curve into Chichester Harbour. Your patience will be rewarded with soft sand and clear seas rivalling the Caribbean (if you squint), plus a row of colourful beach huts for photo ops.

West Wittering, PO20 8AJ
⇌ Victoria to Chichester, then taxi
westwitteringestate.co.uk

INDEX

IMAGE CREDITS

CONTRIBUTORS

Sonya Barber is an east London-based writer and former editor at *Time Out*, *Condé Nast Traveller* and *Ink Travel Media*. She is an expert on the capital – and the author of the very first book in this series, *An Opinionated Guide to East London* – who, over the last few years, has discovered just how much fun there is to be had outside of the city. She spent her pandemic exploring Southern England to research this book. Tough job, eh?

Hoxton Mini Press is a small indie publisher based in east London. We make books about London (and beyond) with a dedication to lovely production and brilliant photography. When we started the company, people told us 'print was dead'; we wanted to prove them wrong. Books are no longer about information but objects in their own right: things to collect and own and inspire.

An Opinionated Guide: Escape London
First edition

Published in 2022 by Hoxton Mini Press, London
Copyright © Hoxton Mini Press 2022. All rights reserved.

Text by Sonya Barber
Copy-editing by Florence Filose
Design by Matthew Young
Production by Anna De Pascale
Production and editorial support by Becca Jones

*To James, the Louise to my Thelma, and little Moon,
who came along for the ride* – Sonya

Please note: we recommend checking the websites listed for each
entry before you visit for the latest information on price, opening times
and pre-booking requirements.

A CIP catalogue record for this book is available from the British Library.

ISBN: 978-1-910566-92-3

Printed and bound by FINIDR, Czech Republic

Hoxton Mini Press is an environmentally conscious publisher, committed
to offsetting our carbon footprint. This book is 100% carbon compensated,
with offset purchased from Stand For Trees.

For every book you buy from our website, we plant a tree:
www.hoxtonminipress.com